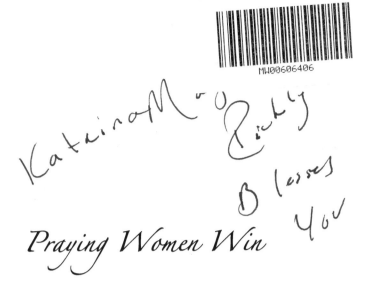

Praying Women Win

2 Chronicles 7:14 — *"If my people, who are called by my name, will humble themselves and pray and seek my face and turn from their wicked ways, then I will hear from heaven, and I will forgive their sin and will heal their land."*

Patricia Clinkscales

Praying Women Win

Published by

Hadassah's Crown Publishing, LLC

Simpsonville, SC

Library of Congress Catalog Number: 2022903900

ISBN 978-1-950894-69-7

All definitions referenced in this book were taken from dictionary.com.

Printed in the United States

This book is dedicated to my husband, Pastor Larry Clinkscales, Sr., who has always been there for me through the good and bad. To my oldest son, Colliness Jones, who was there in my brokenness when I needed deliverance from my pain. To my other two children, Larry Clinkscales, Jr. and Diamoneka Clinkscales Heyward, for trusting me to be there for them. To my late grandmother, Curley Jones, who showed me how to love despite difficult situations.

Love you all dearly.

Praying Women Win

Introduction

Having a prayer life is simply spending time with God and talking to Him about anything and everything. When situations arise, take them to God in prayer and He will lead you and guide you. He's waiting on you to ask Him. He yearns for you to know Him through prayer.

Praying Women Win is more than a personal story of a young woman who originated from Earl Homes in Anderson, SC. I was blessed to overcome many struggles by having a prayer life with God and the unfolding of scriptures that followed. My life has touched the lives of countless people who visited my home.

For the first time, I am sharing my remarkable story in print. In my earnest search for a deeper understanding of God through prayer, I had a profound spiritual experience. An experience that people could not understand and bitterly opposed, yet the Spirit guided and taught me in the face of opposition.

In *Praying Women Win*, I present my testimonies and prayers through the years, revealing that God answers prayers. Understanding God through having a prayer life can change everything about you and your loved ones and anyone connected to you. How to pray is talking to God and allowing Him to talk to you by faith. Your prayer life must be consistent to be effective.

Are you ready to meet God intimately and personally through prayer? Are you willing to listen to His voice? Are you prepared to know Him by praying and seeking His face?

My prayer life was my comfort and strength, and I want the same for your Christian life. My friends, if you are ready to begin a personal relationship with God through praying, God will surpass anything you ever dreamed possible. Pray on!

I was born on September 30, 1960. My new life began on March 7, 1990 when I was 29. On that day, I was born again and accepted Christ as my personal Savior. I have to relive my old life to accept the life God had for me.

This book is especially for prayer when you are going through certain situations and circumstances in life. I also share personal testimonies of experiences that I endured as a new Christian. My goal is to get people to trust God because He has all the answers.

Matthew 6:33 – *"But seek first his kingdom and his righteousness, and all these things will be given to you as well."* As you read this book, remember 2 Chronicles 7:14. My goal is to get you to pray!

When you finish reading this book, I pray that your life will be transformed by the renewing of your mind. Romans 12:2 reads, *"Do not conform to the pattern of this world, but be transformed by the renewing of your mind. Then, you will be able to test and approve God's will – His good, pleasing, and perfect will."*

God's miracles started transforming my life. My prayer life began to change as I prayed daily, seeking God for answers that I would not leave his presence until He gave me a word. Jeremiah 32:27 states, *"I am the Lord, the God of all mankind. Is anything too hard for me?"*

As I started my journal in 1997, I had no clue that I would be writing a book. At that time, my husband was addicted to cocaine and my life was in a downward spiral. Then, the Lord began to answer my prayers and heal my family and me from the pain and agony that we endured.

Praying Women Win

Contents

Chapter 1

My Story

On Saturday, November 15, 1997, I attended a Joyce Meyers
Conference in Atlanta, GA, with some ladies from
Cornerstone Assembly of God. I had not planned to attend,
but my husband insisted that I go. I did not like the way these
ladies acted or their attitudes, but it was really my own
insecurity. I thank God that I decided to go.

During the conference, we began to praise God. Joyce
Meyers told everyone to place their hands on their stomachs,
which is the resting place of the anointing. She said that you
will feel a mighty breaking. As I put my hand on my stomach,
I began to weep uncontrollably. I stood there and heard the
words "Write a journal." Immediately, I thought in my mind
that I could not do this because I was not intelligent enough.
I know that this was due to my insecurity in not knowing
who or what I was and Who I was serving. I could hear the
Spirit saying, "I can help you," so I responded "Okay, Lord"
and started writing my journal.

I remember living with my grandmother, step-grandfather,

two aunts, two uncles, and my two brothers at 6A Earl Homes in Anderson, SC as a child. My mother lived in the same apartment complex, but she was an alcoholic. That is why she felt it best for my two siblings and me to be raised by my grandparents. My biological dad was with my mother until I was two months old, then he abandoned us and moved to Greenville. I never had a real relationship with him, and he only called me on my birthdays.

Growing up, I was a sad little girl due to the abandonment by both of my parents. I could not understand why my mother did not want me to live with her because I saw her every day. Her apartment was across the parking lot and visible from the front door of our apartment.

Around the age of four or five, I recall my step-grandfather waking me up, taking me to the bathroom and having sex with me. I did not understand what was happening because I was a young child, but I remember him saying not to tell my grandmother. You might ask this question, "Where was everybody else who lived in that apartment?" But no one was ever around. My grandmother was out shopping once a week for fabrics because she loved to sew. One aunt was working, and the other was in school because I remember meeting her everyday walking home from school. My uncles were just out in the street, and my brothers were playing sports at the Boys and Girls Club.

I did not understand why my step grandfather told me not to tell my grandmother. I wanted to because I knew something was wrong. The molestation happened on her shopping day when she would be gone for several hours. On those days, she visited a friend who also lived in our apartment complex. After he finished molesting me, he told me to get dressed and I would walk to her friend's apartment. Or if my grandmother was gone shopping, he would make me get out of the house until she returned. The days that I walked to her friend's house, I looked at my mother's apartment and had a strong desire to tell her what was happening to me. But all I could hear was his voice telling me not to tell. It was a mean demonic voice. I had no doubt that my grandmother loved me because when I would get to the apartment where she was, and she would put me between her legs with semen and blood running down my legs. My heart was saying "Why couldn't my grandmother see this or smell the odor of sex on me?"

This abuse happened from ages 5 – 11 years old, until I began menstruating. I would know automatically to come into the house and go to the bathroom after the house was empty. He kissed me, put his tongue in my mouth and blew in my ear as if I wasn't a young child. Then, he had rough sex with me until he ejaculated.

When I started school, I would go to my mother's

apartment every morning to get dressed and for her to comb my hair, thinking why she could not sense what I was going through due to that awful smell of sex that lingered on my young body. At that time, I was very timid, scared, hurt and afraid to share with her what was happening to me. She never asked me about my living conditions and how I was treated, but inside I was screaming, "Help." I noticed on those mornings that a lot of men hung out at her place, and I realized a few years later that she ran a liquor house. I also saw men beating her.

My grandmother would call my mother every week and tell her that my brothers and I were being disrespectful to my step grandfather who I hated with a passion. Our mother was drunk most of the time and beat us with sticks. She put a gun to our heads and told us she brought us into this world, and she would take us out of this world. I would scream at the top of my lungs for someone to help me, but there was no one. She called this discipline, but this was physical abuse.

Living in the Earl Homes was like living in Sodom and Gomorrah. There were drug houses, drug addicts, gambling, hustling, homosexuality, and prostitution. Parents were abusing their children. You could hear their screams from their apartments. Some women operated bootleg hair salons.

People were murdered daily, and the police were always present. There was a large field in our complex, and everything that you could name was happening in it. I saw men, women and even children fighting each other. In that same field, a street preacher came on Sundays for a couple of hours. After he left, the chaos with the cursing and drinking started all over again.

The complex was infested with roaches and rats, and I remember some of the men shooting the field rats with BB guns. We had pigs, cows, chickens, dogs, and cats that we chased through the neighborhood because of a nearby farm. This was a horrible place to live.

After the sexual abuse ended, I buried it in my subconscious, as if it never occurred. I felt like a joyful 11-year-old and played, laughed, and smiled, but I still could not understand what had happened to me. I became flirtatious around all men and craved attention because I thought all men were like my step grandfather and wanted me in a sexual manner. Since I was always around my uncles and brothers who loved me and did not abuse me, I realized that they were not like him.

My step grandfather was a very mean man. He worked from 4:30 am – 1:30 pm. I was so happy when he was not at home because I had the freedom to eat, watch TV, and just be mentally free. When he arrived home, the atmosphere of the house changed. I wasn't allowed to do anything. I could not go in the refrigerator for food or water because he sat there with his foot propped against the door. I had to watch the tv programs that he watched. My grandmother was always in her bedroom sewing, and I can remember running in there, crying and telling her that he would not let me eat, drink, or watch TV. He responded negatively and told me to go to my own mama. My grandmother would holler back to him and say, "This girl is going to hate you."

My grandmother, on the other hand, was always full of love, compassion, and she practically gave me anything that I asked of her. She never worked and was provided for by my step grandfather. There were times that I asked my grandmother for money to go to the store, and she told me to ask him. When I did, he gave me a demonized look, pointed his finger toward my mother's apartment, said, "Go to your mama" and turn up his lips like a pouting child. He eventually gave me the money after my grandmother kept saying, "That child is going to hate you when she grows up."

Although the sexual abuse ended, my step grandfather was now mentally and physically abusing me. There were times when I got very angry at him and disrespectfully talked back. My grandmother called my mother and told her about it, and she would come over to the apartment with switches and sticks and tell him to beat me while she watched. After the beatings, I went back with my mother, and she made me sit in the room as punishment. You might ask since he was so mean and abusive, why did I not live with my mother? Good question because while I felt that she loved me, I did not have control of where I lived.

As I was growing up, I remember a lady named Ms. Ilene who took my friend Laverne and me to her church, Anderson House of Prayer, on Sundays and Tuesdays. Looking back over my life, I know that God had His hands on me. When we were at church, people were constantly praying over us. I thank God for Ms. Ilene planting that seed. After she passed away, we began going to church with Ms. Ruth. My grandmother also took me to church with her. That gave me a love for going to church. Then, there was Ms. Frances Moss who took me under her wing. I truly thank these women for sowing those seeds in my life.

During my teenaged years, at age 13, I began to branch out, and Laverne and I started going to church on our own. Because my grandmother was ill, she stopped attending. We continued to attend Trinity Baptist Church, along with some other neighborhood children. At that time, I became close friends with a girl named Sally who also walked to church with us. I became a Sunday School teacher at age 14. Then, I met a boyfriend, fell in love with him and started having sex with him. Then, instead of going to church, I started going to my boyfriend's house. But I told my grandmother that I was going to church. Sally was always with me as my cover-up. I had another good friend named Sandy who lived across the street from my boyfriend. Her boyfriend and mine were buddies, which led us to become buddies. We saw each other every day. Sally would tell me daily that I needed to stop having sex with my boyfriend because I was going to get pregnant. My teachers at school also told me that I was better than my behavior and to stop running after boys. It was evident to them that I loved boys.

Shortly thereafter, I became pregnant at 15. Then, I felt rejection because I told my boyfriend that I was pregnant, and he told me that the baby wasn't his. He broke up with me. This was during my tenth-grade year in high school, and I was embarrassed, scared, and lonely. I didn't have anyone to tell because of the lack of family support, so I shut down mentally. I went to school and wore big clothes to hide my pregnancy. People would ask me if I were pregnant, but I was in denial and would ask them why or say "no" because I was ashamed. Every day, I rode the bus home from school and closed myself up in my bedroom. I didn't realize that I was in a state of depression. I thought about how I could get rid of the baby without anyone finding out. I even had suicidal thoughts.

Even though I was depressed and dealing with mixed emotions, I knew how to pray because my grandmother taught me. I thank God for the power of prayer. I started praying that God would allow my baby to be healthy. While I was not receiving prenatal care, I ate healthy food. One day my grandmother looked at me and asked me if I were pregnant. Then, she told me that I was pregnant. Next, she called my mother, told her and then my grandmother scheduled me a prenatal doctor's appointment in November of 1975. I became very sick at school one day, but I made it through that day. I knew I was in my ninth month, and when I got home my water broke. I told my grandmother and was taken to the hospital.

When the doctor came out to speak to my family, he informed them that I was in labor. My son was born on October 21, 1975, weighing seven pounds and eleven ounces. My family and friends were surprised and shocked because no one knew how far along I was in my pregnancy. Naming a child at 16 can be difficult because you don't know the meaning of names, but I wanted my son to be very smart and intelligent. I ended up naming him after Dr. Collins who delivered him. I named him "Colliness," which was a variation of my doctor's name.

After I got home from the hospital, I thought I was going back to live at my grandmother's house, but there was no room there. I went to live with my mother in her apartment. My mother felt like a stranger to me because I really didn't know her since we never lived together. She asked me who was the father of my son and I told her his name. She told me to call him and let him know that I had the baby, which I did again. I had already called him while I was in the hospital to ask him about the baby's name. Immediately, his mother called and asked if she and his daddy could come to see the baby. I told her "Yes." She came in with a baby picture of her son, and he and my son looked identical. From that point on, she loved her grandson and would pick him up every weekend. But his dad and I never communicated. God really heard my cry as a teenage mother. As my son grew up, he became an intelligent young boy despite my bad decisions as a teen.

After moving in with my mother, my life became a nightmare. At the age of 16, I was a rebellious teenager. I was drinking liquor because my mother ran a liquor house, giving me easy access. I was also smoking cigarettes and marijuana, and partying seven days a week. I slept around with different guys and shoplifted. I drank alcohol and smoked before I went to school every morning. My friend Laverne's grandmother also ran a liquor house, so she drank too and brought alcohol to school like I did. We both loved to drink and have fun. We attended school every day, but we cut class to drink and hang out with our friends.

It was always drinking, smoking, and fighting during our school days. I was making the wrong decisions and choosing the wrong paths without a sense of direction for my future. I didn't realize that my grades were important, and I was failing my classes due to poor attendance. During my senior year, I had to work very hard to graduate due to my lack of focus and not taking my education seriously. By the grace of God, I was blessed to graduate on May 22, 1978, with my high school diploma, which was the happiest day of my life.

After graduation, I was faced with the decision of which way my life should go. I decided to attend Tri-County Technical College to pursue an associate degree in secretarial science. I went for one year, but still was not focused. My bad decision-making caused me to end up failing my classes. Then, I went to Forrest Junior College also for secretarial science, but I had the same mindset and eventually quit. I found a job in a work training program through Tri-County Tech called Manpower. From that program, I worked various jobs, but I was never content with the positions. I was always searching for something else.

By this time, I was 20 years old. A friend of mine introduced me to a guy from Pendleton, SC, because she was dating his brother. We started dating and I felt like I finally had a boyfriend who would show me love and attention for who I was and not just my body. I fell in love with him and thought he felt the same because some days he told me that we were going to get married. He played with my emotions and bought me things. I totally gave him my heart and fell deeper in love with him. Little did I know that he had multiple girlfriends. While we were dating, I caught him at a hotel with one of his girlfriends, which broke my heart. This caused me to have an emotional breakdown, and I was unable to eat or sleep. I continued to see him despite my hurt and pain. I lost weight since I was not eating. One day, one of my uncles saw me and asked what was going on with me. He noticed my countenance had changed. This made me realize the state of mind that I was in, and that encounter gave me the courage to end the relationship for good.

After ending that relationship, I met Larry Clinkscales through the same friend who was dating his cousin at the time. He was currently married, but not happily so we had an affair. My conscience bothered me because I knew that was wrong, but I was young, broken, confused and tired of still being in love with the other guy.

My spirit was truly confused whether I wanted to continue dating Larry or try to get back together with the other guy. I finally broke up with Larry because he was married, and I reunited with my ex-boyfriend. The relationship did not last. A year later, I reconnected with Larry, and he and his wife were separated, He was living with his mother.

Still looking for love and answers, I called my friend Laverne who was living in New York at the time. I told her

that I was dating a guy named Larry Clinkscales and she said
he was a good catch. I told her that I did not want him
because of my continued love for my ex-boyfriend. After
listening to her, I allowed the relationship with Larry to
continue. I got an apartment and Larry moved in with my son
and me. We lived together for two years, and he divorced his
wife. Laverne eventually moved back to Anderson. She was
dating my brother, and they had a daughter. They lived
together in the same apartment complex with us. They were
both strung out on drugs and alcohol. Our party life was
getting deeper and deeper, and Laverne and I were also
shoplifting everywhere.

One day we decided to steal negligees and wore them the
same night for our boyfriends. A month later, we found out
we were both pregnant. We stopped our bad habits during
our pregnancies and delivered our sons seven days apart.
Shortly after that, we picked our bad habits back up again. At
that time, my baby was four months old, and my oldest son
was 11. Larry and I decided to get married, and he was good
to us. We had a big wedding, and Laverne was my maid of
honor.

After the marriage began, I discovered that Larry was also
a broken man, just like I was a broken woman with no clue
who I was and how to be a wife. He was a drug dealer and a
drug addict, just like I was. We smoked reefers and snorted

cocaine all the time. We drank, also. I could drink a case of beer and still stand up and walk straight. Because of Larry's drug dealing, we always had people around us. My life was spiraling out of control, and this made me realize that I needed to change. I began to seek God again. I watched TV preachers, listened to gospel music, and recited the sinner's repentance prayer. But I would return to my old habits the next day.

When my oldest son turned 13, he became very disrespectful and rebellious to me and Larry, and all three of us would fight physically. His grades started slightly dropping at school. This was a result of the environment that we exposed him to while he was growing up. I sincerely began to seek God for a change in my household because my son was out of control. I still had a close friendship with Laverne who also expressed a change was needed for her and her family's life. God truly has a way of getting your attention when you are sincerely praying and seeking Him. I decided to seek counseling for my son because I felt that he was also depressed. I made an appointment with our family physician. The doctor examined and counseled him. Then, he called me into the examination room and looked at me and said, "Mama, it's not your son. It's you." I replied, "Me?" Then I asked, "What's wrong with me?" He told me that I had to examine myself and that my son was just being a rebellious teenager. He said if he were depressed that he would not be able to function, make good grades and play an instrument in school. Then, I really had to examine my home situation after his evaluation. My son and I left the doctor's office. In the car, he looked at me and said, "Mama, I told you that there was nothing wrong with me. There is something wrong with you." I replied to him that since there was nothing wrong with him that he needed to do better.

The next day I drove Laverne to a doctor's appointment. As we were riding in the car, I began to share with her what my son's doctor had said about me needing help. She said that she also needed help and that she was tired of her life situations. While sitting in the waiting room at the doctor's office, Laverne and I were just staring into space as two broken women. When she was called back into the examination room, I went outside and sat on a bench in front of the office. I looked up in the sky and the sun was very bright. I said, "God, there has to be a better life than this," and I began weeping uncontrollably.

After a while, Laverne came out from her appointment. She said that when she saw the doctor, she was crying hysterically, and the doctor and nurses had to calm her down. That's when our spiritual revelation began. We looked at each other in the car and said again that we needed help. We didn't have a clue where to get help. Laverne suggested that we go to her Aunt Ruth's house. She was a minister. When we were growing up, she was the woman who took us to Refuge Church of God and planted seeds in our lives.

As we entered her home, Pastor Ruth Thompson looked at us and saw how defeated and broken we were. She asked us what was wrong with us, and she could see that life had taken its toll on us. We told her that we were tired of the way life was beating us down, so she began to talk to us about Jesus. We listened eagerly as she shared with us about her relationship with the Lord. That same night, which was a Wednesday, she invited us to Bible study. Of course, we said "yes" and could not wait until 7 pm for the service to begin.

At the service, Pastor Thompson did an altar prayer with us and told us to call on the Name of Jesus. She called it "tarrying for the Spirit." When we left there, we felt like something was still missing and we needed more before we went home. Earlier we had received an invitation to a different church's revival and decided to attend. There, Laverne and I finally surrendered our all during their altar call and accepted Jesus as our personal Savior. This is when our spiritual journey started. Remember, Larry and I were drug addicts and lost, and we both needed Jesus. Two years later, I had a third child.

Periodically, my three children and I visited my grandmother. I was a very protective mom. Before walking in the house, I would tell my children not to look at my step grandfather or go near him. I could see him from the corner of my eyes, and I would grab my children, rushing into the room where my grandmother was. I still had so much hatred, bitterness, and resentment in my heart against him, although at that time his health was deteriorating. All I wanted was an apology for the sexual abuse. After he passed away, I was very happy because at the age of 17, I wanted to kill him. When I attended his funeral, I harbored the same ill feelings toward him and was the first one to burst into tears. I thought that this was the happiest day of my life, that I would never have to see him again. I had waited on this moment for a long time so that I could visit my grandmother more often. I loved visiting her. Little did I know that after his death, I was still not free mentally because I had not been healed emotionally from that terrible ordeal. I was tormented daily from his abuse, as if he were still here on earth. I knew then that God had to heal my heart and soul.

At this time, Laverne and I were attending Mount Olive Pentecostal Holiness Church faithfully. Oh, how we praised God and sought Him more and more. We remained there for about three years and then decided it was time to go back to Laverne's aunt's church, Refuge Church of God. A year after our return, we realized that Pastor Ruth Thompson was a praying woman. We went to church on Tuesdays for Bible study and Thursdays for prayer. It would only be five of us there, but you would think it was 500 because of the spirit - filled service. That is when we learned the power of prayer.

One Thursday night during prayer, my heart was heavy because of my life's trials. I was wailing and sobbing before the Lord. After the prayer, Pastor Thompson stood behind the pulpit and said to me, "Anna (which is what she called me) you cried inconsolably, and God laid on my heart that all five of us should fast and pray for Larry for seven days." So, we fasted and prayed for seven days. The fast ended the day before Good Friday. I invited Larry to church for Easter, but he did not respond. Pastor Thompson called me and asked me to see if Larry would come on Sunday to grill food because we were having a guest speaker. He agreed and came. While he was outside grilling, the guest speaker began to preach about his deliverance from drugs. I realized then that Larry needed to hear this testimony. I asked Pastor to ask Larry to come inside the church because he would if she asked him. She told me that I needed to ask him. We kept debating who should ask him, and she finally did. He came in and the guest speaker was still preaching about drugs and his deliverance. He had an altar call, and Larry went to the altar with his arms outstretched, standing for two hours in that position while the minister continued to preach and give his testimony about his drug deliverance. Finally, the minister stopped preaching and realized that Larry was standing there, surrendering his life over to the Lord. The church began to pray for Larry, and we saw an awesome move of God.

Five years later, I received a phone call from my mother that my grandmother died, which caused my life to go in a downward spiral. I became hysterical and fell on my knees, screaming and asking God why He took the one person who truly loved me. I was hurt, feeling rejected, and mad at God. I began to pray asking Him for strength to make it through this difficult loss. He gave me strength, and I felt in my heart that He spoke to me and said that He would give me the same love that she had for me. Immediately, I got off my knees and went to my grandmother's house to help the family with the funeral arrangements. I felt so much peace knowing that God put His loving arms around me and carried me through this terrible time in my life. Days and nights, I reminisced about the love that my grandmother showed me as a child and young adult, which enabled me to move forward.

After my grandmother's death, I was working on second shift at JP Stevens, but I did not want to be there. I desired to be at home with my children. Even though God had saved Larry, he was still struggling with drug addiction. I also knew that there was something else better for me. I had attended college, but that did not work out. I began to fast daily, asking God which way to go. I took a voluntary layoff a year later, and I knew that was my answer. I was happy just being home and drawing unemployment benefits that only lasted for six months. During that time, I did my cousin and sister-in-law's hair.

One day after doing hair, I told my son who was now 19 that I needed to find a job. He looked at me and asked, "Mom, why don't you go to beauty school?" I didn't have confidence in myself and replied, "Beauty school? I'm too old to go to beauty school because I am 35 years old." He then said, "But Mom you just finished doing hair." His statement resonated with me and made me remember doing my grandmother's hair when I was 10 years old. She told me back then that I had "growing hands" and prophesied that I would do hair and that I would also have a cleaning service because I cleaned very well. As a teenager, she rewarded me every Saturday with her credit card for cleaning the house. I was very happy to go shopping with my friends. I began to pray and ask God for direction. After seeking Him, He laid it on my heart to go Alpha Beauty School.

The cosmetology program lasted nine months. After I graduated, I decided to do hair at my house. My mother was one of my clients and would get her hair done once a month. I noticed at her appointments that she always had a sad countenance. I prayed and asked the Lord what was wrong with her. One day she said that she had overheard me telling

someone that I hated my step grandfather. This made her
open up to me and share her life story. She told me that she
had watched an episode of Oprah who talked about being
sexually molested as a child. She realized that she had
endured the same thing at the hands of my step grandfather
when she was only four or five years old like I was. I told her
about how he sexually abused me, and she apologized to me.
She said that if I had told her, she would have blown his head
off. I asked her if she ever told my grandmother about her
abuse, and she said that she did. But grandmother did not
believe her. I feel in my heart that my grandmother knew she
was telling the truth, but she was in denial because this was a
taboo subject in her generation. My mother also confessed
that she had been an alcoholic for over 50 years. She went to
bed drunk and woke up drunk trying to deal with the trauma
of that sexual abuse. She said that she was tired of the
drinking and was ready to change her lifestyle. That led me to
witness to her about the change that God made in my life. I
invited her to church with me on Sunday.

At that time, I was attending Cornerstone Assembly of
God. We picked my mother up and she was ready. He
preached about salvation and how God can help you
overcome the pain of a broken heart. He also said that God
can heal all of life's situations. You could see relief on her
face as the pastor gave the altar call. She immediately went to

the altar, and I saw her with her hands lifted, surrendering to God. Larry was an altar worker for the church. That day, he was standing at the altar. He was the one who prayed for her and led her to the Lord. I was praising God. When my mother got in the car after service, she was so happy, and her countenance had changed. I could see a spirit of peace on her. I knew then that the Lord had lifted the heavy burden off her that she had carried for many years. All God asks us to do is to surrender to Him.

From that day forward, every Sunday she attended church until she became ill years later. One Sunday she said to me, "Ann, I tried to visit my old friends that were still drinking, but I realized that was my past and that I was ready to move forward." Then I said to her, "God's hands are upon you. You asked Him to take those desires away from you and He did. He does not want you to go back to your old life." This transformation in my mother showed me that my God is awesome and powerful. He tells us to ask and believe, and He can do anything but fail. My mom called me every day talking about the abuse, and I was able to minister to her. I realized, however, that I still had unforgiveness in my heart towards her. I had to ask God to help me forgive her for neglecting me and allowing me to suffer the abuse at the hands of my step grandfather. I asked God to *"create in me a clean heart and renew a right spirit within me,"* according to Psalm 51:10. I went to my mom and asked her why she let me stay with my grandparents knowing the abuse that she suffered. She stated that she felt that because she ran a liquor house and had men in and out, that it was a safer environment with them. She said that she was selfishly living her life and thought that was the best route to take. She asked for my forgiveness. I wished I could say that I forgave her instantly, but it took time after much prayer and fasting.

One day, God gave me a scripture to help me through the days, months, and years that I struggled to forgive her. Isaiah 41:10 says, "So do not fear, for I am with you; do not be dismayed, for I am your God. I will strengthen you and help you. I will uphold you with my righteous right hand." God kept His Word and made me stronger until I was able to go to my mother and tell her that I forgave her.

Due to years of alcohol drinking and not taking care of herself, my mother got sick. She had diabetes, muscular dystrophy, and several other illnesses. Because I had forgiven her, I was able to be around her before she died on January 22, 2008. I helped take care of her by transporting her to doctor appointments and running errands for her. When she was unable to live alone, I had to place her in a nursing home. I visited her and took her to the ministry activities held on Tuesdays.

One particular Tuesday, we were at a singing event and my

mother was very happily looking up and gazing toward the ceiling. She asked me several times when Jesus was coming to get her and I answered, "Dot, I don't know. That is between you and God." I sensed something must have happened that day that connected her to Jesus. The next day, I received a call that my mother had passed away, and I know now that she was seeing angels the prior day. I was at peace about her passing.

I always sought God daily about my life. Every day, I asked Him to heal the broken pieces because I was still very bitter concerning my biological father. I had a longing in my heart to reconnect with him because I did not have a relationship with him. He had abandoned me as a child. I recalled a conversation with a co-worker who did not grow up with her father either. She saw him for the first time at his funeral and I did not want that to happen to me. This was when I was in my 20's that I decided to try to find my father.

Based on what my mother had told me, he had his own detailing car business in Greenville, SC. Larry and I went to Greenville, and I stopped at a phone booth. I looked up his name in the Yellow Pages and he was listed as B's Auto Detail Shop. I wrote down the address and we went there. On the way there, I asked Larry how we planned to introduce ourselves, and he said that we would tell him that we needed our car detailed. Once we arrived, a young man came out to our car, and I asked to talk to the owner. Larry talked to the owner about the car and told him that we were from Anderson. I was trying to make myself noticeable because my father had told me that if he ever saw me again, he would immediately recognize me. He saw me, but he did not seem to know who I was even though he reacted to the fact that we were from Anderson like he had a previous connection there. This hurt me deeply that he did not recognize me. He told Larry to bring the car back on Monday for detailing.

As my father walked away from the car, I yelled out "Mr. B, you don't know who I am?" He stared at me and then I said, "I'm your daughter." He replied, "You look just like your mama." I told him what he told me in a phone conversation when I was 17, that he would recognize me whenever he saw me. He asked me if I needed anything other than getting the car cleaned and I told him, "No." We said "goodbye" and left his shop.

As we were driving a few miles down the road, I decided to call him and ask him for some money as a test, since he asked me if I needed anything. We stopped at a phone booth so I could make the call. His wife answered the phone. I did not know it was his wife at the time, but I saw her at his shop when we were there. He got on the phone, and I said, "Mr. B., this is your daughter and you asked me if I needed anything." I told him that I needed money. He asked me how much and I told him "money" but did not give him a specific amount. He told me that he would send me money on Monday through Western Union because we spoke on a Friday evening. I asked him if he were lying because I told him that my mother said that he told lies. He said, "No, no, no," that he would send it to me. I checked Western Union on Monday, Tuesday, and Wednesday and nothing was ever sent. I called him back on Wednesday and asked him what happened, and he said that he never consulted with his wife about me because she did not know that I existed. He could not send me any money without jeopardizing his marriage and his family. After he said that, I was in a rage. I said horrible things to him, told him to forget that I existed and that he didn't ever have to worry about me contacting him again. I felt a spirit of rejection and was embarrassed and humiliated after reaching out to him.

At the age of 35, I contacted my father again because I found out that I had two brothers and one sister. I wanted to meet and get to know them. He asked me why I wanted to meet them, and I said that we all have children who need to get acquainted. He responded angrily and said, "My children will never accept you. Let bygones be bygones." I said to him in a calm manner, "Sir, why are you so angry? What have I done to you to make you so angry because I am your daughter?" I remember telling him that he was the reason that his family did not know about me. He was in a rage and got louder as he spoke to me, trying to convince me that my siblings would not receive me. I asked him, "Sir, have you accepted Jesus as your personal Savior?" He was offended by my question. His response was that he had been in church all his life and that he sang in the choir. He wanted to know why I asked him that. I told him because he was so angry and mean. I finally ended the phone call and said "Sir, bye. I will be praying for you" and hung up the phone. I began sobbing and asked God what I did to deserve the rejection of my father and his lack of love for me. Immediately, the Holy Spirit gave me peace and comfort and let me know that He would never leave me nor forsake me. He would always be a Father to me.

After seeking God about this, I was still determined to find my siblings without his assistance. A few months later, I received a hair referral for a lady whose last name was the same as Mr. B's. When she came to my house to get her hair done, I asked her questions and if she knew my father. She said that he was her brother-in-law. She gave me my siblings' names and information on where they lived. She told me that my sister lived in a different state. I decided that I would try to contact my sister first. I called my dad's shop again and spoke to his wife but did not identify myself. I told her that I was trying to reach her daughter about a personal matter and left my information for her to contact me.

About two weeks later, I received a call from my sister. I gave her the shocking news that I was her sister. She was speechless for a few minutes and finally responded, "Why are you just now contacting me?" I told her that I had been trying to get to know them for years. But our dad said that he never informed the family about me, and he did not want confusion. I told her that he was very mean when he spoke to me, and she said that he was just old and talked loudly. I did all the talking and she did not ask me any questions, so she did not seem interested in getting to know me or ever contacting me again.

Next, I tried to find my brothers, but to no avail. Years later, my daughter met her future husband who was from Greenville. His mother asked her who her relatives were, and my daughter told her that she had a grandfather who lived in Greenville. After she told her his name, it was determined that she knew him and my siblings. I did a search of my brothers again and located one of them. I called him and he too was in shock after I told him who I was. His response was "What do I do now?" I told him that we needed to meet so our children could get to know each other. We didn't set a date to meet before the conversation ended. I called him a year later in 2017 to see if he was ready to meet and he told me that he would be in Anderson the following week. He was supposed to call me, but he never did. He texted me on Mother's Day of that year and again on one occasion in 2018, but we still have not met. My prayer is one day that victory will be won and that I will meet my siblings.

In April 2017, I received a phone call from my maternal brother who lives in Greenville, and he stated that my father had passed away. I did not know how to feel. My emotions were all over the place, ranging from sadness to indifference since I really didn't know him. I was indecisive if I should attend his funeral or not, which might have given me a chance to meet my siblings. I was also very angry and disappointed with my father because he did not make this right with my siblings and took this to his grave with him. I decided not to go because I had a prior engagement on the day of his funeral. I called my brother who told me that he was going to the funeral. He brought me an obituary. I saw a family picture on the obituary, which allowed me to see how my siblings look. I became very emotional looking at the picture and questioned why he never let me meet my siblings in his lifetime. God reminded me of the scripture Psalm 27:10, which reads "When my father and mother forsake me, then the Lord will take me up." This reassurance gave me immediate comfort and peace of mind. I knew then that I had to let my resentment towards him go.

My desire is to be healthy mentally, physically, and

spiritually. I didn't think in a million years that God would use me to write a book. I began to write daily in my journal from my heart, taking breaks on the weekend. I'm always meeting people and met a young lady at the gym who had just written a book. She told me about her book, and I began to laugh because God has a sense of humor. I felt like He was speaking through her to me to also write a book. She told me who to contact and said that they would help me with the process of what to do and how to do it.

On the first of January every year, I fast and pray, asking God for a Word for the year. This time in 2018, His Word was very significant to me because He spoke to me and said, "I'm bigger than anything." Then, He said "It's time to a write a book." My response was "Oh." I thought about it since I already kept a journal, and all I had to do was put it in book form. I was never good at writing and using proper English even while in school, but I just wrote. The kids made fun of my grammar, but I always liked to write because I knew one day that I would be able to help someone. Then, I said to myself, "Ann, you can do this," but I knew I couldn't do it in my own strength.

The scripture that came to me was Philippians 4:13 which reads, *"I can do all things through Christ which strengtheneth me."* As I prayed, God gave me instructions as to how to put this book together. My experience with the Lord, after accepting

Him as my personal savior, is that He will give me what to say to His people. He is so amazing! When you talk to Him, He will talk to you. All the drama that I had to endure gave me my life story to write this book, and I pray that it will help everyone who reads it by giving them courage to let go and let God. Life is good with Jesus being the center of it. If you put God first, your life, which is like a puzzle, broken and scattered, will be put back together by Him because He wants us to be whole. I pray that you will seek the Lord and not let your past dictate your future. If God can set me free, He is fully able to do the same for you and your family. I know that some have had worse experiences than I have, but we all have the same God who can do anything but fail. He wants you to be happy and to live life abundantly. God always has a ram in the bush. I want to thank Tracy Robinson for helping me put this book together. May God richly bless you.

My first emotion as God was bringing me out of my ordeal was joy. I had gotten so tired and frustrated with my life that I began to search for healing. I can remember getting very angry one day, needing answers about life. I took a drive in my car. As I was driving, I saw a tent and a sign for church service that night. I know everyone is not familiar with outdoor tent meetings. I was very skeptical about going back to attend, but remember I am seeking the Lord for answers. When I got home, I told Larry about it and asked him to go with me. He said that he didn't want to go. Of course, I knew that he did not understand at that time what I was going through. I was tired of being tired, so I went alone. I left home that night weary in well doing, but still needing answers. When I arrived at the service, there were only five people in attendance. They sang three songs and I tried to get into the service, but it was boring. Physically, I was there, but mentally I was not because I was bombarded by the cares of life. Offering was collected before the preaching, and I didn't want to give any money. I looked in my purse and reluctantly decided to give $20. As I was putting the money in the collection plate with a sad countenance on my face, the usher spoke to me and said, "Ma'am I don't know what you are going through, but don't let nothing or no one steal your joy. When you give to God, you give it cheerfully." Immediately, I began to smile. He said to me, "That's right. Keep that smile on your face." When I got home that night, I said to Larry, "God has given me joy. From this day forward, my life will never be the same again because God has spoken to me."

That is when my journey started in 1991. God has done a great work on me. I pray that everyone who reads this book will be blessed, set free, and delivered. I pray God will transform your life so that you won't even recognize yourself anymore. You will be a new creature in Him. I know it can happen because that's what He did for me. Don't take my word but try Him for yourself because God is bigger than any situation or problem in this world. The scripture says in Matthew 6:33, *"But seek first his kingdom and his righteousness, and all these things will be given to you as well."* Every day, I start with prayer and God always gives me a scripture. In the next pages, I will share the scriptures and prayers that God gave me for my healing process.

Chapter 2

Everyday Living

Matthew 6:11-12 – *"Give us today our daily bread. And forgive us our debts, as we also have forgiven our debtors."*

Every day we wake up, our prayer should be "Thank you, Lord" for another day. If you are reading this, you have the ability to see. You have a lot to be thankful for because He woke you up today. Jesus watched over you as you slept and did not let any harm come upon you. Every day should be a happy day. Psalm 118:24 states, *"The Lord has done it this very day; let us rejoice today and be glad."*

Prayer

Lord, I thank you for another day. Thank you for life, health, and strength. Today I, _____, put all my situations in your Hands. Thank you, Jesus, for working it all out. I command this day to you. Lord, I pray that the Father of glory may give unto you a spirit of wisdom and knowledge for this day. Amen.

Chapter 3

Strength

Philippians 4:13 – *"I can do all things through Christ who gives me strength."*

When I think about God's strength, I think about having a child at the age of 16. Every day I asked God to help and strengthen me to carry a child because I was a child myself. Psalm 46:4 says, *"There is a river whose streams make glad the city of God, the holy place where the Most High dwells."* My God, our God, will see you through. Trust Him.

Prayer:
Lord, you said you would be my strength. My very present help in the time of trouble. Lord, I'm trusting you to see me through, according to Psalm 46:1. Amen.

Chapter 4

Joy

James 1:2-3– *"My brethren, count it all joy when ye fall into divers temptations; Knowing this, that the trying of your faith worketh patience."*

These verses talk about joy in trials. Joy doesn't come easy during trials. During difficult seasons of life, it's so much easier to get carried away by worry and anxiety, but God gives us a better way. Even in our struggles, we can experience pure joy in choosing to silence those inner voices and trust God on a deeper level than we ever have before. Is it easy? Definitely not! Is it worth the fight? Every single time. As I stated earlier, we need to hear from God and give every situation to Him in prayer. When we cast our cares over to Him daily, we will see Him turn it around. *"The joy of the Lord is our strength,"* says Nehemiah 8:10.

When I was pregnant, I prayed every day and asked God for a healthy and intelligent child. My son was born on October 21, 1975. That day was bittersweet for me. I did not know what to expect as a teenage mother, but the minute I heard him cry I began to smile and oh what joy I felt in my heart. The thought of killing my child had left my mind and love had come. I can truly say in dark times, God can give you great joy.

When I first accepted Jesus, I still did not know how to walk in the joy of the Lord. Years ago, I was going through different situations in my life. I remember coming home one day and passing a site of an upcoming tent meeting at 7 pm that night. When I got home, I told Larry about it and that I would be attending. I went with a very heavy heart ready to give up on life and my marriage. During the offering, a man approached me and said to me as I was giving my money, "Whatever you do, do it with joy." I smiled at him, and he said, "That's what I'm talking about. Don't let anything steal your joy." I continued smiling and have been smiling ever since that day because the joy of the Lord is my strength. Psalm 28:7 says, *"The Lord is my strength and shield; my heart trusts in him and he helps me. My heart leaps for joy, and with my song I praise him." "Every day is a day that the Lord hath made. Be glad and rejoice in it."* (Psalm 118:24)

Prayer:

Father God, thank you for my joy. I have and will go through different things in life, but your Word always encourages us.

"The joy of the Lord is our strength," says Nehemiah 8:10. I know if you took me through the last situation that you will also take me through this. Help me as I go through to smile and never lose hope. I know you have all things worked out. Thank you, Lord, for the joy, no matter what the situation is. Amen.

Chapter 5

Seeking After God

Matthew 6:33 – *"But seek first his kingdom and his righteousness, and all these things will be given to you as well."*
Isaiah 55:6 – *"Seek the Lord while he may be found; call on him while he is near."*

God will prove himself to you if you seek Him. God will draw you closer and closer to Him. As a young girl, I knew there was a God, but to draw close to Him took going through a lot of trials and tribulations. God has never failed me, and He won't fail you either. You will learn to say, "through it all I've learned to trust in Jesus." So, my sisters and brothers, seek the Lord and call on Him. He won't let you down!

Prayer:

Lord, I know you have all things in Your hands. Thank you, Lord, because my righteousness is like dirty rags, so I seek you for your righteousness. Amen.

Chapter 6

Humbling Yourself

2 Chronicles 7:14 — *"If my people, who are called by my name, will humble themselves and pray and seek my face and turn from their wicked ways, then I will hear from heaven, and I will forgive their sin and will heal their land."*

You will hear this verse a lot. This is one of my favorite scriptures in the Bible. The word "humble" means "meek," "deferential," "respectful," and "submissive." When you humble yourself before God, it is highly submissive. He is the King of Kings and the Lord of Lords. When you submit yourself to God, He will show you great and marvelous things that you know not of.

1 Peter 5:6 — *"Humble yourselves, therefore, under God's mighty hand, that he may lift you up in due time."*

Timing is the key. We must wait on Him. I guarantee He will come through.

Prayer:

Father, help me to be obedient to Your Word. Help me to humble myself before you daily. I know if I am obedient to what you tell me to do, I will hear from you, my Savior. Amen.

Chapter 7

Hearing from God

Mark 4:9 – *"And he said unto them, He that hath ears to hear, let him hear."*

Sometimes hearing from God consists of doing what's right or simply asking yourself what would God do? It's His Word that leads. He will guide you unto all truths. Reading the Bible allows Him to speak. Carrying my son at the age of 16, I would tell myself once he was born, I was going to kill him. Throughout the pregnancy, I wanted to take something to get rid of him. Inside of me, I wanted to do the right thing. Now, I know it was God because I prayed every day for my son. I can remember saying, "Lord, give me a smart, intelligent, and healthy child," and God did just that. I know God was leading me on what to do and how to do it. "What a friend we have in Jesus."

Prayer:
Lord, I pray in Jesus' Name that you give me ears to hear You and only You. A stranger's voice I will not hear. Amen.

Chapter 8

Peace

Isaiah 26:3 – *"Thou wilt keep him in perfect peace, whose mind is stayed on thee: because he trusteth in thee."*

Oftentimes in the Bible I think about God's great peace. This is how awesome our God is. When Jesus and His disciples were on the boat and a storm arose, Jesus was asleep. Mark 4:37 says, *"And there arose a great storm of wind, and the waves beat into the ship, so that it was now full."* The disciples were nervous and afraid. Mark 4:38-29 states, *"And he was in the hinder part of the ship, asleep on a pillow: and they awake him, and say unto him, Master, carest thou not that we perish? And he arose, and rebuked the wind, and said unto the sea, 'Peace be still.' And the wind ceased, and there was a great calm."*

So, what is Jesus saying? If I can tell the sea to be still, your situation is small. You have to speak to whatever is going on in your life and say, "Peace be still." It works. Try Jesus. He will give you the peace that *"surpasses all understanding"* (Philippians 4:6-8). *"Be careful for nothing; but in everything by prayer and supplication with thanksgiving let your requests be made known unto God. And the peace of God, which passeth all understanding, shall keep your hearts and minds through Christ Jesus."*

Prayer:

Father, I pray in Jesus' Name that I learn to walk in peace and not in pieces. Lord, keep my heart and mind stayed on You. You said if I do that, You will keep me in perfect peace. Lord, when I get weary, help me to look to You. I know there is nothing worth my worries, but all things are worth my praise. I thank You now for my peace. Amen.

Chapter 9

Fear

Isaiah 41:10 – *"Fear not, for I am with you; Be not dismayed, for I am your God. I will strengthen you. Yes, I will help you. I will uphold you with My righteous right hand."*

Fear was the driving factor that changed my life. Going through my many situations, a spirit of fear gripped me. I had been praying for this area of my life because every time I left home, I had to have someone with me. I can remember wanting to go to the store but being too afraid to leave my house. One day, I needed to go to Walmart and asked my husband and children to accompany me, but no one wanted to go. I went alone and talked to God, asking Him for strength. I prayed all the way there. When I got inside the store, I recall passing two ladies who were discussing someone being in the hospital. I could hear the Holy Spirit telling me to pray for that individual who was sick. Of course, I did not because of the spirit of fear. I quickly picked up my items from the store and went home.

When I got home, I did not have any peace about what transpired and felt guilty for my disobedience. Larry was in the yard washing cars. I told him what happened, and he gave me a puzzled look as to why I just didn't do it. I went back to Walmart to the section of the store where I had seen those ladies and found out that one of them worked there. I told her that I had overheard her conversation with the other lady. I asked if she minded me praying and she responded, "Oh yes, my mother-in-law has been in a coma for two weeks." As I began to pray, she said that her mother-in-law believed in the power of prayer. I touched her hand and prayed a simple prayer. "Father, I pray in Jesus' Name that you will heal her body. In Jesus' Name. Amen." I did this with fear and trembling. I asked her if she would call me and give me an update about her mother-in-law. She said "Sure," and we exchanged numbers. The next day she called and said, "This is the lady from Walmart. I wanted to let you know that after you prayed for my mother-in-law, her nurse called me and said that she opened her eyes and asked for food."

This incident was when I realized that God had a calling on my life for intercessory prayer. After this I was able to go places alone. To God be the glory. Every day I would find scriptures on fear and meditate on them. Then, I started my ministry to pray for others. I don't know when my fear left. All I know is that I was obedient to what God asked me to do. So, my prayer for you is found in 2 Timothy 1:7 and reads, *"For God hath not given us the spirit of fear; but of power, and of love, and of a sound mind."*

Prayer:

Lord, I know you did not give me a spirit of fear. You have given me a sound mind, so I pray now for the spirit of fear to leave me. Amen.

Chapter 10

Wisdom

James 1:5 – *"If any of you lack wisdom, let him ask of God, that giveth to all men liberally, and upbraideth not; and it shall be given him."*

Because I grew up not having a mother and father in my life, when I became a Christian, I wanted wisdom. I can remember praying every day asking God to give me wisdom in every aspect of my life and looking up scriptures. I would not do anything until I sought wisdom. Sometimes, that meant going to my pastor or elderly saints, and I still would pray about the situation. So, in life, things will occur, so always seek wisdom.

Prayer:
Lord, I know what Your Word says, that if I ask You will give me the desires of my heart. So, I'm asking now for wisdom in this situation. Amen.

Chapter 11

Understanding

1 Corinthians 10:13 – *"There hath no temptation taken you, but such as is common to man: but God is faithful, who will not suffer you to be tempted above that ye are able; but will with the temptation also make a way to escape, that ye may be able to bear it."*

Thinking about my past and all the things that I endured, I could not understand why. That was my question as a babe in Christ…why I had to go through molestation, abandonment, growing up fatherless and motherless, teenage pregnancy, loneliness, and physical and mental abuse. I remember praying about these things every day. God began to minister to me after a lot of my pity parties. He began to tell me that He was going to use me to help others. I asked Him how I would be able to help others because I was messed up. During my prayers, God gave me scriptures like Genesis 50:20 which states, *"But as for you, ye thought evil against me; but God meant it unto good, to bring to pass, as it is this day, to save much people alive."* When you need understanding, you must go to

God in prayer. Proverbs 3:5-6 says, *"Trust in the Lord with all thine heart; and lean not unto thine own understanding. In all thy ways acknowledge him, and he shall direct thy paths."*

Prayer:

Matthew 6:9-11 – *"After this manner therefore pray ye: Our Father which art in heaven, Hallowed be thy name. Thy kingdom come. Thy will be done in earth, as it is in heaven. Give us this day our daily bread."*

Chapter 12

Love

John 3:16 – *"For God so loved the world that He gave His only begotten son, that whosoever believeth on Him should not perish, but have eternal life."*

As a young girl growing up, I did not have anyone to talk to or to tell me that they loved me. It was very difficult. Love was not demonstrated to me. All I knew was hurt and pain. Love to me was having sex. That was the only form of love I saw. I felt my grandmother loved me. But with me not knowing the love of Jesus, it was a shallow love. When I had my son at the age of 16, I told myself that I was going to love him. But I had to ask myself "What is love?" because I didn't know how to love. I knew that God was love.

I can remember when my grandmother died. I felt like she was the only one who loved me. When I got the phone call from my mother telling me that my grandmother had passed away, I got down on my knees and started wailing like a baby. I could literally hear God saying to me, "The same love your

grandmother shared with you, I want you to show to others."
I immediately got up off my knees and went to the family's
house. I began working on her obituary. That's my God's
strength. I was able to help my family members cope with
their grief. Love is powerful; love is God; God is love. The
same love God has for us, we need it for one another. Again,
"Pray without ceasing," according to 1 Thessalonians 5:17.

Prayer:

Lord, I thank You for giving Your only Son to die for me. I
ask You today to help me believe in Him. Help me to know
of His unconditional love. If I was the only one on this earth,
I could say, "You did it all for me. Thank You, Lord, for
Your everlasting love." Amen.

Chapter 13

Finances

"Give and it shall be given unto You, good measure pressed down, shaken together running over shall they give into your bosom. For with what measure ye mete, it shall be measured to you again." Luke 6:38

In 1998, I was attending Cornerstone Assembly Church. I was very devastated because my home and finances were out of order. We were on the verge of losing our home. Larry and I didn't know what to do. Our level of faith was very low. My oldest son was in college, and we had a lot of bills and debt. I can remember at this time, we only had one car, a red, Volkswagen which needed major repairs and had holes in the floorboard. We could see the road when we drove it, and my daughter was scared to ride in it because she thought she would fall through it. We kept driving that car until the tires literally fell off. It would not go in reverse, and we would have to push it backwards whenever necessary. Lol!

One day, Ms. Jo Beth McDonald gave me a ride home from church. When I got home, I shared with her that we were going to lose our house and she said, "Pat, I rebuke that in the Name of Jesus. You will not lose your home. The devil is a liar." I felt the Holy Spirit within me leap for joy. From that day on, I began to pray, asking the Lord to save our home. I had to stand on God's Word because He allowed us to build this home, so I could not allow my flesh to fail. I declared and decreed every day. Our God is good. He won't let us down. Today, in 2021, we are still living in the same home. To God be the glory! I learned the more I give, the more God gives to me. Thirty years later, I am writing this book to help others know that God has our backs. Believe that!

Prayer:

Help me Lord to believe what Your Word says about giving. Help me to be obedient to Your Word. The more I give, the more You will give to me. Amen.

Chapter 14

Children

Proverbs 22:6 — *"Train up a child in the way he should go: and when he is old, he will not depart from it."*

I talked about having my oldest son when I was 16 years old. I was a child trying to raise a child. My mother and his paternal grandmother had to do it. I was too busy "sowing my wild oats" as the older generation would say. When my son reached his teenaged years, things got bad. He became rebellious and did things I could not believe, but I did not give up on him. He began to change through much prayer. He graduated from high school and went to Livingstone College in Salisbury, NC, to study business. Now, he has his master's degree in business. When I look at him, I know that God can do anything but fail. So, parents be encouraged. If we give our children back to God and always pray for them, He will turn them around. That is exactly what He did for my other two children. The scripture above is one that I stood on raising them 12 years later. I give all the glory to my God and honor to my husband Larry for the training of our children.

Our children were trained to pray, read the Word, and go to church, and disciplined in love like Proverbs 13:24 says, *"Whoever spares the rod hates their children, but the one who loves their children is careful to discipline them."* We tried to do everything a Christian family would do. Our children are also testimonies because they did unexpected things when they became teenagers. It made me reflect on when I was a teenager, and the scripture came to mind. 1 Corinthians 13:11 states, *"When I was a child, I talked like a child, I thought like a child, I reasoned like a child. When I became a man, I put the ways of childhood behind me."*

In this scripture, God is letting us know that children are not adults and have not grown up to maturity. They will make plenty of mistakes. I know I made my share. Did I learn from them? Some I did, and some I did not. Some of them, I'm still learning how to grow up from them.

Parents, always think about what you did when you were young because you were not perfect. You may not have done what your children are doing, but you did something. Stop being so hard and arguing with them. Listen to them. One day, they will grow up and guess what? You will laugh about it. So, chill out and love one another. My children did things, but now we get along. Growing up is good and sometimes it comes with pain. But God's got it.

My two youngest children are college graduates. My daughter has a bachelor's degree in education from the University of South Carolina and a master's degree in education from Clemson University. She teaches sixth grade. My son, Larry, Jr., has a bachelor's degree in animal science from Tuskegee University and now works in business. I always give glory to God. He will turn our children around in His time. Just ask Him!

Prayer:

Father, I put my children in Your hands. I know I have done my part. I release them to You. They are Your children. I give them to You in Jesus' Name. Amen.

Chapter 15

Grief

"Blessed are those who mourn, for they will be comforted."
Matthew 5:4

Grief always causes deep sorrow when one of your loved ones passes away, something tragic happens or someone breaks your heart. Some people will say "let them go" or "let it go." I say everyone grieves differently depending on the relationship that you had with that person, or sometimes we have issues that we hold onto that make us grieve. When my grandmother passed away, I thought my whole world was gone. After I received the phone call that she had died, I ran into my bedroom and got on my knees. I cried bitterly saying "Lord, help me! Help me!" I cried all day long. I went to sleep that night and woke up still crying.

As I continued crying, I realized I had to be there for my family. Then I began to pray. Listening to the voice of God makes a big difference. I could sense in my spirit what He was saying to me. "Patricia, the same love your grandmother had for you and for others, I want you to show the same love to everyone who comes in contact with." Immediately, I began to reflect on her overwhelming love for me as a child and as a teenager.

After praying, I knew that my family needed me to write the obituary and handle the other affairs. God gave me so much peace, joy, and love. I was so full of His grace. So, I say to whoever is reading this chapter on grief, ask God for His strength. He is there to help you with any grief that you are carrying. You may want to give up. Remain faithful to God, and He will remain faithful to you. Be strong in the Lord, and He will leave the 99 to rescue you. Do not let anything steal your joy. God will hide you under His wings. Although you may not have a great beginning, you will have a great finish.

Prayer:

Today, Lord, I am grieving. Please give me comfort and peace that I need to carry on. I trust You. I know I can do this with Your help. I ask you now for strength. Amen.

Chapter 16

Worrying

"Casting all your care upon him; for he careth for you." 1 Peter 5:7

Singing, praises and melodies will always get you through worrying. I often think about what God has brought me through. This book lists the things I've been through and yes, worrying was one of them. I had to learn that worrying is not from God. As I begin to think back over the 23 years that I have been saved, I know that God has brought me through many things. So quietly I would say to myself, "If God brought me through addictions to drugs and alcohol, surely He can bring me through this. So, I say to you today, whatever you're worrying about, think on the worst things that have happened to you. If He delivered you from that, I know He can do this. Be encouraged because God will not let you down. I don't care what it is. There is nothing worth your worry, but all things are worth your praise. Put some praise and worship music on and relax. Give it to God. He loves you and He doesn't want us to worry.

During my daughter's first year of college at the University of South Carolina in Columbia, SC, God helped me deal with excessive worry. My husband discussed with me that our daughter needed a car. I immediately started worrying, knowing that she was so young, in a city larger than Anderson, SC and had to get on the interstate to travel. We went to a dealership, although we didn't have any money to buy a car. God showed us favor. We found a car and explained to the car salesman our situation, and he was able to arrange for us to get the car. After we got home, Larry said, "We need to take the car to our daughter in Columbia," and I said, "No, she can't have this car." I went to pray and while praying, God spoke to my heart immediately. He said that the same God that kept our daughter safe while driving in Anderson would keep her safe while driving in Columbia. That reassurance released me from worrying. The next day, we took the car to her, which made my daughter rejoice in happiness. I was at peace knowing that God would protect her.

Prayer:

Lord, You tell us in Your Word to cast all our cares upon You. Today, I come to You, casting all worrying and frustration upon You because You care for us. Lord, I thank You now because there is nothing worth my worries, but all things are worth my praise. Amen.

Chapter 17

Direction

Proverbs 3:5-6 — *"Trust in the Lord with all thine heart: and lean not unto thine own understanding. In all thy ways acknowledge him, and he shall direct thy paths."*

Which way shall I go? What shall I do? I need direction in my life. Writing this book is an indication of direction. Praying and asking God what to do, what to write about, who to call, what to say. Go here. Go there. This is my whole life. My life has been directed by God, only by asking Him. He knows the way we should take. The Bible is a road map leading us to Jesus. Your life is a puzzle and only God can put the pieces together, if you allow Him. Some doors open and some doors close. You may want to go left, and God says go right. This is life. God is just like the GPS you use in your car, which tells you where to turn. God also allows U-turns. Romans 8:28 KJV says, *"And we know that all things work together for good to them that love God, to them who are the called according to his purpose."* Jeremiah 29:11 NIV states, *"For I know the plans I have for you,"* declares the Lord, *"plans to prosper you and not to harm you, plans to give you hope and a future."* So now again, I would have never thought I would be going in this direction, but God will lead you and guide you which way you should go.

Prayer:

Father, You said in all my ways if I acknowledge You that You will direct me. So, I come to You for direction. You said You will never leave me nor forsake me, so I come boldly to You asking You for direction. Give me an ear to hear You. Thank You for leading me. Amen.

Chapter 18

Praying for a Mate

"Delight thyself also in the Lord: and he shall give thee the desires of thine heart. Commit thy way unto the Lord: trust also in him; and he shall bring it to pass." Psalm 37:4-5 KJV

At the time when I got married, I did not know who God was. But I knew how to pray. My desire was to be married, even though I did not have a good example of marriage. My grandmother and step grandfather were married for 40 years, but it was an ungodly marriage with him sexually abusing my mother and me. Due to the molestation, I was afraid to give my heart to a man, although I was giving my physical body to men. My God is awesome, and He always looks beyond our faults and sees our needs. I wasn't looking for a mate, but He knew my son needed a father-figure in his life. I met Larry through his cousin, but he was married at the time. I knew him from high school and actually had a crush on him. I called my friend Laverne and told her that I had met him. She told me that she had hung out with his wife and knew that Larry was a good man. I was still in love with someone else, but I went out with Larry a couple of times. My conscience started bothering me because he was married, and I did not want to date a married man. So, I broke things off.

A year later, my other relationship ended, and Larry was separated from his wife and had moved back in with his mother. We began dating again for a year and a half, and Larry finally divorced his wife. After his divorce, we really became close. He and my son had a good relationship at that time, and I saw how well they interacted with each other. Four years later, Larry asked me to marry him. Of course, I said, "Yes." As I look back over everything that I had to endure in my life, I know that God had Larry ordained for me as He told Jeremiah that He knew the plans for him. So now, I know that God has a plan for each of our lives. If you are looking for a mate, continue to pray without ceasing and do not settle. Be encouraged and wait on the Lord because God wants the best mate for you. *"For the vision is yet for an appointed time, but at the end it shall speak, and not lie: though it tarry, wait for it; because it will surely come, it will not tarry."* Habakkuk 2:3 KJV

Prayer:
Let this be a prayer for you. Lord, help me to love You first and fall in love with You. Then, You said You will give me the desires of mine heart. Amen. Let it be so. Selah

Chapter 19

Healing

Isaiah 53:5 – *"But he was wounded for our transgressions, he was bruised for our iniquities: the chastisement of our peace was upon him; and with his stripes we are healed." KJV*

The first miraculous healing that I can remember at age six is my grandmother's testimony that God had taken the taste out of her mouth for alcohol and delivered her from alcoholism. I could not understand that until I became addicted to drugs and alcohol. Remembering her testimony, I knew that God could do the same for me. I sought Him and prayed for deliverance. He heard my prayer just as He heard my grandmother's prayer. I had children and wanted to be a good example for them. According to Acts 10:34, *God is not a respecter of persons.* What He does for one, He will do for us all.

Prayer:

Father, I thank You for healing me from the top of my head to the soles of my feet. Every cell in my body is healed. My heart and mind are healed. I am healed from all struggles and all addictions. Everything about me is healed – my thoughts, my ways, my actions, and my marriage. Thank You for Your healing hands being upon my children, my family and me. I believe this Lord by faith. Amen.

Chapter 20

Compassion

Ephesians 4:32 – *"And be ye kind one to another, tenderhearted, forgiving one another, even as God for Christ's sake hath forgiven you."*

Growing up in my state of mind, I did not know how to show compassion. Not being touched or loved made compassion hard for me. When I got married, Larry said to me, "Patricia, you don't love people." My mindset was "Why do I need to love or show compassion to anybody?" First of all, I had to be healed in this area of compassion because all I knew was how to take advantage of others. But you know when you allow God to control your life you start becoming like Him and your mindset will change. You will be loving and more compassionate to others. You do not want to treat people the way you were treated. You want to do better. As I began to get closer to God, I prayed and asked Him to heal that area of my life. Matthew 7:12 – *"Therefore all things whatsoever ye would that men should do to you, do ye even so to them: for this is the law and the prophets."* After reading and meditating on

God's Word daily, my heart began to change, and I continued to get better. I want to see others happy. So, if you are struggling with compassion, do what I did and ask God for help. Let love conquer every situation.

Prayer:

Lord, help me to show compassion to people as You show to me. I know that Your grace is sufficient for all of us and Your mercy endureth forever. Thank you, Lord. Amen.

Chapter 21

Employment

3 John 1:2 KJV – *"Beloved, I wish above all things that thou mayest prosper and be in health, even as thy soul prospereth."*

Our heavenly father is very interested in you and desires the very best for you. I had been working for JP Stevens in Clemson, SC for 10 years when I decided to take a layoff to be a stay-at-home mom. During my time of unemployment, it was great until the unemployment benefits ended. I had to ask myself a question: "what I was going to do?" No money, no job, and my husband was only working part-time four days a week. I had to trust God, so I prayed and asked Him for direction. My oldest son was home from college at that time and I shared with him that my UI benefits had ended. He said to me that I should go to beauty school because I had just finished doing a neighbor's hair. At that time, I had a spirit of fear because I was 35, and I thought I was too old to go to school. However, my mind reflected on when I was growing up and had a desire to do hair. My grandmother always told me that I had a gift of doing hair and cleaning.

After praying and seeking God, I made the decision to go to cosmetology school, and our God came through for me. I graduated from school and now am a licensed cosmetologist. I also have a cleaning business. To God be the glory! Always pray and ask God to lead you!

Prayer:

I thank you, Father, for supplying my need for employment according to Your riches in glory by Christ Jesus. I believe that it is done. Amen.

Chapter 22

Broken Hearted

Matthew 11:28–30 - *"Come to me, all you who are weary and burdened, and I will give you rest. Take my yoke upon you and learn from me, for I am gentle and humble in heart, and you will find rest for your souls. For my yoke is easy and my burden is light."*

The definition of a broken heart is "Used in reference to a state of extreme grief or sorrow, typically caused by the death of a loved one or the ending of a romantic relationship." I experienced a broken heart many times during my life with the deaths of my grandmother and mother and from bad relationships where I gave my heart to any and everybody. In the Old Testament, the word "heart" is mentioned 800 times with more than 200 times dealing with one's thought life. The motions and wellsprings of life that motivate and mold us are what the Bible calls the "heart." Solomon told his son in Proverbs 4:23 KJV to *"Keep thy heart with all diligence; for out of it is the issues of life."* Proverbs 23:7 says, *"For as he thinketh in his heart, so is he."* Proverbs 4:23 says, *"Keep thy heart with all diligence, for out of it flows the issues of life."*

My biggest heartbreak has been through people. People walked in and out of my life. You need to know what category to put people in because some people are seasonal, and some are in our lives for a lifetime. God's Word and His love can help you get through the heart break that does not feel good. Spending time reading specific Bible verses about being broken hearted allows us to be intimate with God. Through prayer and petition, He can solve the issues in your life. Some people may think you have to be settled in your faith for many years for God to heal your heart, but all He needs for us to do is what is stated in 1 Peter 5:7 KJV – *"Cast all your care upon him; for he careth for you."*

Prayer:

Lord, help us to keep our hearts and minds stayed on You. Isaiah 26:3 KJV states, *"Thou wilt keep him in perfect peace, whose mind is stayed on thee: because he trusteth in thee."* I bring my broken heart to you. I thank You that you will not put more on me than I can bear. Thank you, Lord for strengthening me and healing me in, Jesus' Name. I believe that it's done. Amen.

Chapter 23

Lost Your Way

Isaiah 53:6 — *"We all, like sheep, have gone astray, each of us has turned to our own way; and the Lord has laid on him the iniquity of us all."*

Life brings ups and downs. You may say that I have more downs than ups, but that's not true unless your life is in your own hands. When I was making my testimony doing things I shouldn't do and going places I wanted to go, I lost my way. As I grew older and began to seek God, I learned that if I prayed and let Him lead me, I wouldn't get lost. There are times in life that we need to go right, and we go left. It's okay. God allows us to make U-turns. Just continue to pray and let God lead you. Learning His voice is important. Listening to what God is saying will help us tremendously. So, remember to pray for God's leading and all things will work out. Where Jesus leads you, follow Him.

Prayer:

Father, help your children. We all have fallen short. Help us always remember that you love us unconditionally, so I pray that you continue to draw us closer to you. I thank you now for the Holy Spirit that continues to draw us to you. You said that you would never leave us or forsake us. Amen.

Chapter 24

Confidence

Philippians 1:6 — *"Being confident of this, that he who began a good work in you will carry it on to completion until the day of Christ Jesus."*

Growing up with no one to trust brought me much grief. I did not have confidence in myself or others, so this left me hopeless and wondering who was out to get me. I had my guard up at all times, praying and seeking God asking Him to take full control of my life. As I began to walk with Him daily through my trials and errors, great confidence came to my life. I talked about many tribulations I had to overcome, but this situation happened to me. I had to learn how to trust and have confidence mainly in Christ, that He would bring me out. I had to learn how to walk. I can remember I was praying, asking God to help me. I was so afraid to walk in front of people. I woke up one morning and God told me to put my right foot in front of my left, and that day I began to walk, meaning I started walking out of the insecurity caused by the things that had triggered me to this point. Every day was a brand-new day. I realized I was somebody. I did not have to be afraid. My confidence began to come little by little and precept by precept. Our God is good. I don't care what it is. He has us.

Prayer:

Lord, I pray in Jesus' Name for confidence. I put my trust totally in You. Help me to look to You, the Author and Finisher of my faith. Amen.

Chapter 25

Hurt

Nahum 1:17 – *"The Lord is good, a stronghold in the day of trouble; he knows those who take refuge in him."*

The definition of hurt is "to cause physical pain or injury." Hurt can be hurt feelings, emotional wounds, distress, pain, and broken hearts. All of these are forms of hurt. I want to deal with the feelings of hurt. God gave us all feelings, meaning we all can hurt, whether it results from mental or physical wounds. It's how we handle them. They hurt me so I want revenge to hurt them back, so now you will be going through a lifetime of hurting people because they hurt you. Hurting people hurt people. This is a true saying. I believe my step-grandfather was abused, so hurt people hurt people. So, what someone did to hurt him caused him to take revenge upon himself. I believe God will heal you from yourself. I believe God will heal you from all forms of hurt. He surely doesn't want us to go around hurting others, so we have to pray in every area of our lives. God says in Romans 12:19 to *"Avenge not yourselves, but rather give place unto wrath; For it is written, vengeance is mine; I will repay, saith the Lord.”* From now on, remember to deal with the hurt. It is what it is, but you have to let it go. Give your broken pieces to God and let Him heal you. He will. Selah

Prayer:

Lord, I know You hear me when I cry to You for help. I ask that You heal my hurts. You said if I come to You that You would not cast me out, so I come boldly to You. Heal me Lord from all my hurts. Amen, and it is so. I believe it.

Chapter 26

Weary

"And let us not be weary in well doing: for in due season we shall reap, if we faint not." Galatians 6:9

The older generation would say, "I wished I knew earlier in life what I know now." I can truly say, "Okay, now I understand what they were saying." Going through different situations in life and hitting bumps in the road, you learn. If it did not happen to you, how would you have learned? I can admit some things in life are rough, not knowing what to do or who to consult. When I was pregnant with my son at the age of 16, I was weary. I did not have a relationship with God. I had to learn to get into the Word and read scriptures pertaining to my situation. I learned that crying is not the answer unless you are crying out to God. Most of the time when you call others you find that they are weary themselves. I learned to call on Jesus according to Psalm 46:1 which reads, *"God is our refuge and strength, a very present help in trouble."* So, from now on go to Him. Talk to God. He will always be there. He's our strength, so don't be weary. Sing songs. Get into the Book of Psalms. There is Power in the Name of Jesus.

Prayer:

Help me Lord, when I am weary, not to think about myself, but give me the opportunity to think about others. Let us do good to all people especially to those who belong to the family of believers. Amen.

Chapter 27

Fear

"Fear thou not; for I am with thee: be not dismayed: for I am thy God: I will strengthen thee: yea, I will help thee; yea, I will uphold thee with the right hand of my righteousness." Isaiah 41:10

The Lord walks and talks with me and tells me that I am His friend. God will be a friend to you, but you must gain a relationship with Him. It's like having a friend that you call and talk to daily. Life brings different obstacles. When fear grips you, it can be hard to break. My sister-in-law Laverne always says, "You have to be tired of being tired." That is a profound statement. I was tired of the spirit of fear on me preventing me from being able to walk and talk and to leave the house. God said to me one day "I want you to go fishing." I asked Him, "Fishing for what?" He said, "Fishing for souls." Remember, I'm broken and fearful and yet He tells me to go fishing. So, I answered Him, "Okay. Where do I fish and what do I need?" He said, "I already have a bait on the hook. You go and get them." I said "Wow, okay." So, I started going to the track at Westside High School every Sunday morning to walk. My goal was to win souls through fishing.

While walking around the track, I stopped and started talking to a man about the Lord. I found out that he was a backslider. From out of nowhere, a dog appeared and started chasing me. I was terrified. The man said, "The Blood of Jesus." Immediately, the dog left. Fear had gripped me, but my protector was there. That's when I learned through this man the power of the Blood of Jesus and to plead It over fear from then on. God used this man in his backslidden condition to help me because He said He was married to a backslider. Fear comes from the evil one. Whatever your fear is, speak life over yourself and quote Philippians 4:13 which states, *"I can do all things through Christ which strengtheneth me."*

Prayer:

Lord, I know you got me. You have me in the palm of your right hand. You said that you would never leave me nor forsake me. I will take you at Your Word. Your Word, Jesus, is a light to me. I ask you now to remove this fear from me. In Jesus' Name. Amen.

Chapter 28

Married

"And above all things have fervent charity among yourselves: for charity shall cover the multitude of sins." 1 Peter 4:8 KJV

To know how to love each other, you and your spouse first need to know how to love yourselves. God is love. The word *marriage* is when two come together to become one. My husband and I have been married for 35 years. Boy did this take much forgiveness and much prayer. We both had to learn because we had trust issues. I had to learn that we are becoming one day by day. It did not happen all at once. I also had to learn that we are very different and opposite from one another. He couldn't change me, and I couldn't change him. God had to do the work. We trust Him through His Word. Once I learned that concept, I started praying more for myself and putting Larry in God's hands. It worked. Try it. Through much prayer and letting God work, I started seeing changes in us. This is left up to the couple because all marriages are different. Some may require counseling, which will show you yourself. Learn now or later. Fall in love with God first and then with your spouse.

Prayer:

Lord, I know that this is very important for marriages because marriage is the unification of two people. No one is perfect in a marriage. There will be times that a husband or wife will fail each other. I ask for help, Lord, in those situations, to remember God's definition of love and know that if we love each other deeply, that love covers a multitude of faults. Amen.

Chapter 29

Anger

"Be ye angry, and sin not: let not the sun go down upon your wrath:"
Ephesians 4:26

Life issues can cause anger. As a child, I was molested, which made me angry, bitter, and sad. I grew up wanting to kill my step grandfather who had violated me. I had to turn my anger around through prayer and the Word of God, and I had to forgive him. I had to release it so God could turn it into joy. I had to trust God with this. It was not easy, but I had to learn that this was not my battle. It is the Lord's. Daily, I read 2 Chronicles 20:15. I prayed and asked God to help me. I started thinking positive thoughts. "This is not mine. I'm happy. I'm not angry. I'm joyful."

Prayer:
Lord, I thank You for *what the devil meant for evil You have turned it around for Your good.* Genesis 50:20 Amen.

Chapter 30

Hope

"Be strong and of a good courage, fear not, nor be afraid of them: for the Lord thy God, he it is that doth go with thee: he will not fail thee, nor forsake thee." Deuteronomy 31:6

Losing hope can be very difficult to deal with. Having a child out of wedlock at the age of 16, I did not know how I was going to make it. But I knew there was a God. I prayed daily for the strength to have my child because many days I wanted to terminate the pregnancy. God gave me the hope and desire to keep him. I know His hands were upon my son and me. There is hope in God. Trust Him.

Prayer:

God, I thank You. When I was ready to give up, You stepped in right on time. You are my God, my hope, and my peace in the midst of the storm. I love you, Lord. Amen.

Chapter 31

Forgiveness

God says to forgive those who harm you. In Galatians 3:13, it tells us *"Forbearing one another, and forgiving one another, if any man have a quarrel against any: even as Christ forgave you, so also do ye."*

This scripture was very easy for me to understand what God is saying. I had unforgiveness and hurt in my heart due to my mother abandoning me as a child and being molested by my step grandfather. I had to pray daily. At times, I hated them. I asked the Lord why this happened to me. Over a period of time, I started praying for God to mend my broken heart. It happened. I had to let it go. I don't know when, but I know it happened. Then, the love of God started flowing through me for them. *"Our God is faithful and will never leave us or forsake us."* Hebrews 13:5

Prayer:
Lord, I thank You for Your forgiveness. You forgave me, so I have to forgive others. I forgive _____ who

have hurt or harmed me. I give this to You. In Jesus' Name. Amen.

(You may have to pray this repeatedly until you believe it.)

Chapter 32

Relationships

"Be careful for nothing; but in every thing by prayer and supplication with thanksgiving let your requests be made known unto God. And the peace of God, which passeth all understanding, shall keep your hearts and minds through Christ Jesus." Philippians 4:6-7 KJV

People will walk in and out of your life. We have to let them go. Letting go is one of the hardest things to do. It is easy to hold onto people, but we must trust that our God has something better in store for us and greater than our past mistakes. When we realize that God is in control, we can stand still and be strong. Let go and keep moving on until His work is performed.

Prayer:

God, I know You sometimes allow people and situations to build us up and help us grow in faith in preparation for Godly relationships. Lord, You have us and want us to also have a deeper relationship with You. I love You Jesus, for You know what is best for us. Amen.

Chapter 33

Friendship

"A man that hath friends must shew himself friendly: and there is a friend that sticketh closer than a brother." Proverbs 18:24

Friendship is very valuable. If you have one good friend, value them. I have been friends with my sister-in-law since we were children. I did not know that she would eventually become family. She is still my best friend, my ride or die. We go through many ups and downs, but we have remained friends. We have each other's backs and value our friendship. I have had many to come and go in my life. Some go and some stay. My friend and I always say that our friendship was ordained from God. If you are in a friendship and can't trust that person, that is not a true God-sent friendship. If you are looking for a friend, first pray and ask God to send you a true trustworthy friend. He will honor that.

As a cosmetologist, I do hair for all ages. I remember one day, I was doing a young girl's hair who was in the first grade. She told me that she did not have any friends in school. I began to pray with her that God would send her a friend. She is now 21 years old. I saw her recently and she told me that she found a friend shortly thereafter and they are still friends to this day. I told her "To God be the glory." When God does anything, it is done.

Prayer:

I pray now for everyone who is going through trust issues of any friendships that have caused some kind of hurt. Lord, I know you are a healer of broken-hearted people, so my prayer is for whoever is reading this book at this time that they will *"Look unto Jesus, the Author and Finisher of our faith; who for the joy that was set before Him endured the cross, despising the shame, and is set down at the right hand of the throne of God.* (Hebrews 12:2) Lord, I give you my hurt that developed during this friendship, and I thank You for peace. I know you will work this out. In Jesus name. Amen.

Chapter 34

Anxiety

"Be careful for nothing; but in every thing by prayer and supplication with thanksgiving let your requests be made known unto God."
Philippians 4:6 KJV

Anxiety is defined as "a feeling of worry, nervousness, or unease, typically about an imminent event or something with an uncertain outcome." Life's issues, such as losing a parent, child, spouse, job, etc., can cause anxiety. Whatever the situation, we must keep pressing on and not give up because God is in control. Philippians 4:13 KJV says, *"I can do all things through Christ which strengtheneth me."* Through the death of my grandmother and my mother, the rebellion of an out-of-control child, and husband addicted to drugs, I suffered with anxiety. I had to seek God. I Peter 5:7 instructs us *"to cast all of our anxieties on Him because He cares for us."*

Prayer:

Lord, I know I can't do anything about the way my life is going, but You gave me life. Job 33:4 says, *"The Spirit of God hath made me, and the breath of the Almighty hath given me life."* So, I give all this anxiety to you, Lord, and I thank you that I am free from all worries. There is nothing worth my worries, but all things are worth my praise. Amen.

Chapter 35

Intimacy

Enjoying intimacy is an issue for a lot of couples. Intimacy means "closeness in a private cozy atmosphere." We must first have an intimate relationship with God and then with each other, which is what I had to learn. Couples sometimes start taking marriage for granted. Things happen in relationships that cause divisions. The marital relationship needs to be consistent. Touching, talking, looking at one another, being together sexually, and doing things together keep your relationship intact. Learn to complement each other. This must be done on a regular basis. Due to my step grandfather molesting me, I did not desire intimacy. I had to pray and ask God why I had to be intimate with my husband and how to do so because sometimes I did not want to be. This is how I knew I needed healing. After giving all my hurt to God and asking Him to restore me, He did. It was definitely a process for me. Sex is good because God ordained it for marriage. 1 Timothy 4:4 says, *"For everything God created is good, and nothing is to be rejected if it is received with thanksgiving,*" So now when I experience intimacy with my husband, it is "hallelujah, thank You Jesus" because He delivered me from my lack of desire. Healing is from God because He loves us so and only wants the best for us.

Prayer:

I pray for my brothers and sisters that are reading this. I pray in Jesus' Name that You will give them the desire for an intimate relationship with You and with each other. Lord, whatever You made is good. I pray that you will allow God to do a work in you and your spouse. I know that everything will be alright if we continue to trust God. I pray that you will fall in love with Jesus, Who is our first priority. God will teach us how to love. I pray that you draw close to God. He will draw close to you, and you will draw close to one another. Amen.

Chapter 36

Addictions

My God is a deliverer. I don't care what the addiction may be - drugs, alcohol, sex, pornography, etc. Interacting with a person who has an addiction can influence you also. Twenty-five years ago, my spouse was addicted to crack cocaine. At that time, I felt addicted mentally because of him. There is nothing too hard for our God. This addiction will take you places that you do not want to go and cause you to do things you would not normally do. John 10:10 says, *"The thief comes only to steal and kill and destroy; I have come that they may have life and have it to the full."* The devil meant to come in to destroy my husband, but God had another plan. Larry had to call on the Name of Jesus, and God miraculously healed him. Although God had done the work on Larry, he still fell a few times until he made up his mind that he no longer wanted to live that lifestyle. Proverbs 24:17 says, *"For a righteous man may fall seven times and rise again."* Our God is good. Call on Him. Ask Him to heal you from any addiction that you may be facing.

Prayer:

Lord, help my sisters and brothers who are dealing with addictions in their lives. I know you can do it. Hebrews 12:1 says, *"Therefore, since we are surrounded by such a great cloud of witnesses, let us throw off everything that hinders and the sin that so easily entangles. And let us run with perseverance the race marked out for us."* God is able and will heal all afflictions. Trust Him and He will never fail you. Amen.

Chapter 37

Peer Pressure

Being a follower can lead to peer pressure. Knowing who you are will help you to stay focused. By not changing your attitude, your behavior can transform to those of influencing groups and individuals. Peer pressure can be hard due to our desire to be loved by someone or a part of something. When I was younger in school, not knowing who I was, I began to follow my friends, or they were following me. I stayed in trouble, skipped school, smoked weed, drank alcohol, and was promiscuous. I did it all until I realized who I was and what the devil was trying to do to me. Really, I am a leader, but I did not know I was supposed to be leading people in the right direction. But God. Repentance is the key, asking God to come into your heart. That's when things began to turn around for me. Revelation 3:20 KJV says, *"Behold, I stand at the door, and knock: if any man hear my voice, and open the door, I will come in to him, and will sup with him, and he with me."*

Prayer:

Lord, help me to follow after Your standards. Help me to seek after You. Everything You do is good, so help me so I can help others. Amen.

Chapter 38

Death

How do we deal with death? The death of loved ones is hard to accept. I faced it many times with the death of my grandmother, step grandfather, and my mother. This was not easy, but death is a part of life. Everyone must die. When my mother passed away 13 years ago, it was bittersweet for me. Some days I cried and some days I was happy. It was sad because she was my best friend. The love that she had for my family was incredible, and she would do anything for my children and me. At the end of her life, she was very sick, and I had to place her in a nursing home because she needed around-the-clock care. Going to see her always devastated me because I hated to see her suffering. I remember asking God to heal her or to take her home to heaven. She was so ready to go. She would ask me sometimes when I visited her at the nursing home when was Jesus coming to get her. I would answer that I didn't know, but I told her that He was coming. Two weeks later, my mom died. So, I was happy knowing that God heard my prayer when she died. Of course I was sad, but peace covered me knowing she was with the Lord.

I say to anyone reading this now that everything is going to be alright. God says in His Word in Ecclesiastes 3:1-2 KJV, *"To everything there is a season, and a time to every purpose under the heaven: A time to be born, and a time to die; a time to plant, and a time to pluck up that which is planted."* After I read those scriptures, I realized that it was her time to die. I learned from this after losing my mother to do your best here on earth. My mother was saved and ready to go. Her work was completed, and it was my time to continue to plant good seeds.

Ephesians 6:8 KJV reads, *"Knowing that whatsoever good thing any man doeth, the same shall he receive of the Lord, whether he be bond or free."*

Prayer:

Father, I pray in the Name of Jesus that we will not let the fear of death grip us. We trust you with our life and know that you will give us the strength to deal with death. We know that our loved ones are in a better place. Help us to let go by putting our grief and sorrow in Your Hands and giving us the assurance that everything will be alright. Every day I will give my pain, my worry, my hurt, and my grief to You. Psalm 46:1 KJV states, *"God is our refuge and strength, a very present help in trouble."* Psalm 23:4 KJV says, *"Yea, though I walk through the valley of the shadow of death, I will fear no evil: for thou art with me; thy rod and thy staff they comfort me."*

Chapter 39

Money

Years ago, I was afraid to give to God. I was broke, disgusted, and afraid to spend money that I did not have. God spoke to me one day and said, "Every $20 that you spend, I will give it back to you." I said, "Wow, you would do that for me?" and in my heart I could hear Him say, "Of course." Sometimes you have to try the spirit by the spirit. I quoted 1 John 4:1 every day, that "I would never be broke another day of my life" and through this, I learned the more I give the more God gives back to me.

After I accepted Christ as my personal savior, I started giving 10% of my income. One particular pastor said, "Money doesn't belong to you; it belongs to God." That concept affirmed that God wanted to be in control of my money. Giving to God has gotten me out of debt.

"Give, and it you will be given to you. A good measure, pressed down, shaken together and running over, will be poured into your lap. For with the measure you use, it will be measured to you." Luke 6:38

Once I learned this, I began to trust God with my money.
I began to give, give, give, give and God blessed, blessed,
blessed me to put my three children through college. I can't
tell you all that God has done because of the giving, so I
encourage you today to give. Give until it hurts and watch
our God give it back. Malachi 3:10 says *"Bring ye all the tithes
into the storehouse, that there may be meat in mine house, and prove me
now herewith, saith the Lord of hosts, if I will not open the windows of
heaven, and pour you out a blessing, that there shall not be room enough
to receive it."* God is God. He will not lie. Take Him at His
Word.

Prayer:

Lord, help me to trust You with my money and to know that
it is not my source, but You are. Help me to give
unconditionally and wait on You to come through for me
because You will never fail me. I need Your will to be done in
my life. I love You, Jesus. I am convinced that if I obey Your
Word that You will pour out Your blessings. Amen.

Chapter 40

Teen Pregnancy

The Word of the Lord says in *Proverbs 22:6 KJV* *"Train up a child in the way he should go: and when he is old, he will not depart from it."*

Being pregnant at the age of 16 was very difficult for me. I was in love with my son's father, but he denied that he was the father after I got pregnant. This caused me to separate from everyone. I found myself lonely, depressed, and isolated because I did not have anyone to go to and talk to about my situation. I was embarrassed and hid my pregnancy for nine months while attending school, not telling anyone. Some of my classmates asked me if I were pregnant and I would say "No." I can truly understand now the scripture about training up a child in the way he should go because my grandmother instilled in me how to pray.

As time passed, I stayed in my room until the next day and prayed daily for the Lord to allow my baby to be healthy and brilliant. I ate healthy and my grandmother who I was still living with provided me with balanced meals. I feel like she had an idea that I was pregnant. She finally realized it when I was nine months because of the changes in my body. She told me that I looked pregnant, which I didn't deny. Once she learned of the pregnancy, she made me a doctor's appointment. However, I went into labor at school a few weeks before the appointment date. I came home sick from school and told my grandmother that I wasn't feeling well. She called my mother, and I was taken to the hospital. I was in labor. My son was born later that day and my family was in shock. All they could say was "How could this happen?" Today, I still give God the glory for what He did for me at the age of 16.

What I say to parents is to communicate with your children. Always know where they are and the company they are keeping. I did not have an engaged family who was concerned about my whereabouts and who I was with, so I was able to do whatever I wanted and ended up getting pregnant. I pray for you in Jesus Name that as parents you are watchmen for your children. Your relationship with them is especially important when they are teenagers, and they really need you due to peer pressure in the world. Pray for them and love on them because they need you. Do not abandon them, which is what happened to me. I was looking for love in all the wrong places.

What I say to teenagers is to stay focused. Do not let anyone use or abuse you for your body. Your body is precious, so keep it pure for your future mate. If you need guidance, find a trusted individual to assist you. Do not isolate yourself because "no man is an island." Pray to God because He is there when you feel no one else is. He is omnipresent. Your relationship with God is more than life itself.

Prayer for Teenagers:

Lord, I surrender my life to You. Help me to focus on my relationship with You and not on ungodly associations that cause me heartache and pain. Help me to be still and know You as my personal savior. Amen.

Chapter 41

Abandonment

As I sit here writing, I thought about the word *abandonment*. The definition is "having been deserted or left out or alone, forsaken." As I talked about myself at the age of 16, all these words came to me. I truly identified with the word *forsaken*, because as a child and teenager I was forsaken. I stated earlier in the book that I was abandoned and left alone as a child, which caused life to take a turn for me. Having a relationship with God will keep you on the right path. When I gave my life to Christ, I found that to be true. Everyone on this earth has a reason for being here. You have to find your purpose. *"For I know the thoughts that I think toward you, saith the Lord, thoughts of peace, and not of evil, to give you an expected end."* Jeremiah 29:11 KJV

Prayer:

Deuteronomy 31:6 KJV – *"Be strong and of a good courage, fear not, nor be afraid of them: for the Lord thy God, he it is that doth go with thee: he will not fail thee, nor forsake thee."* God is with us at all times. He is omnipresent. Amen.

Chapter 42

Prosperity

Prosperity is "defined as a successful, flourishing, or thriving condition." I can remember being an entrepreneur as a child. I had a business in school selling bubble gum to my classmates for five cents apiece. My grandmother sold candy apples and candy bars, which was my example. My business allowed me to always have money. I began working at a sewing factory at age 20. I got married at age 25 after the birth of my second son, and I had a third child, my daughter, at age 27. I would go to work miserable every day because I wanted to be home with them. I fasted and prayed, asking God for direction for my life. I ended up working there for 10 years before He opened the door for me to leave. My oldest son was in college and came home one particular weekend to visit. I shared with him about my misery on the job and he encouraged me to go to school. My answer was that I was 35 years old and too old to go back to school. The next week at work, management asked if any employees wanted to take a layoff. I raised my hand, although I was very nervous, but I could hear my son saying to go back to school. After I was laid off, I was not sure where to go for schooling. My son gave me the idea of beauty school for cosmetology. I questioned him "Beauty school?" and he said, "Yes." He had just witnessed me doing the neighbor's hair across the street. See, God can use anyone He chooses to lead us on the right path. I thought about that and prayed about it. God spoke to me and confirmed that I should attend beauty school, which was the plan for my life. God has a plan for our lives, and we don't always see the gift because of many distractions. We are talking about prosperity and for years I did not believe in myself and my gift, but now I see it. My gift made room for me and now at age 60, I have been a successful hairstylist for 25 years. To God be the glory. God has given us many gifts and talents. I also have a cleaning service. My grandmother prophesied when I was 10 years old that I was good at cleaning and that I had a gift for doing hair. God has truly blessed me to be prosperous.

Prayer:

I pray for prosperity in your life and that God will provide your needs. I pray for wealth and success for you and your family. Seek the Lord in all your ways, and He will direct your paths. Amen.

Chapter 43

Battle of the Mind

"From the end of the earth will I cry unto thee, when my heart is overwhelmed: lead me to the rock that is higher than I."
Psalm 61:2 KJV

The battle of the mind is something that I did not mention in my story. When I was carrying my son at the age of 16, my mind was overwhelmed. I thought, "A baby – what am I going to do?" At that time, I did not know about hearing strange voices in my head. Now I know I was hearing the voice of the devil because they were evil thoughts. The enemy was telling me that no one knew that I was pregnant and for me to kill my baby after he was born by throwing him in the lake. But remember, I was praying for God's help while I was carrying him. I now realize that what the devil meant for evil, God will turn it around for His good. Genesis 50:20 KJV says, *"But as for you, ye thought evil against me; but God meant it unto good, to bring to pass, as it is this day, to save much people alive."* If the voices you are hearing are not good, then they are not of

God. Our God is awesome. He always encourages us and does not discourage us. A couple years ago, there was a bracelet that people wore with the letters WWJD that stood for "What would Jesus do?" Always ask Jesus what you should do so you can choose to do the right thing.

Prayer:

Lord, I know you hear me when I pray. Help me to know Your voice and not to listen to a strange voice that is not of You. You are a good God. Strengthen my mind to think and act like You. Amen.

Prayer of Acknowledgment

Dear Lord, I want to thank you. If it had not been for the Lord who was on my side, where would I be? Thank you for this opportunity to share my testimony and prayers. I thank you for your love, kindness, grace, and your mercy that brought me this far. Thank you for hearing my cries throughout these years. Thank you for giving me the strength to share the miracles and the things that you have done for my family. I pray that you will allow the people that you have chosen to read my story to receive a blessing and that hearts will be changed. I pray *2 Chronicles 7:14* over your people. Thanks again for my family, and a special thank you to Ms. Ilene and Ms. Frances Moss for touching and blessing my life. I love these people dearly. In Your Name. Amen.

I want to thank Hadassah's Crown Publishing, LLC for giving me this opportunity.

About the Author

For the first time, Patricia Ann Jones Clinkscales is sharing her remarkable story in print. In her earnest search for a deeper understanding of God through prayer, Patricia had a profound spiritual experience. This was an experience that people could not understand and bitterly opposed, yet the Spirit guided and taught her in the face of opposition.

In *Praying Women Win,* Patricia presents her testimonies and prayers through the years that God answers prayers. Understanding God through having a prayer life can change everything about you and your loved ones and anyone connected to you. How to pray is talking to God and allowing Him to talk to you by faith. Your prayer life must be consistent to be effective.

Are you ready to meet God intimately and personally through prayer? Are you willing to listen to His voice? Are you prepared to know Him by praying and seeking His face?

Patricia's prayer life was her comfort and strength, and she wants the same for your Christian life. She says, "My friends, if you are ready to begin a personal relationship with God through praying, God will surpass anything you ever dreamed possible. Pray on."

The author can be contacted at patclinkscales@gmail.com.

Made in the USA
Columbia, SC
29 March 2022

Professional Pharmacy

1409 Main St. Anderson, SC 29621

864-224-3581
Fax: 864-231-6240

Your prescription has been sent to Professional Pharmacy. A representative will contact you within 1 to 2 business days. If you do not receive a call within the time frame, please call us at **(864) 224-3581.**

Please have your prescription insurance card and the following information readily available.

1. RX Bin or Bin number (usually 6 digits long)
2. RX PCN if applicable
3. Identification number
4. RX Grp or Group number
5. An e-mail address for the tracking number
6. Payment information

We are open on:
Monday - Friday 8:30AM to 6:30PM EST
Saturday 9AM to 2PM EST

Please call us with any questions or concerns
at (864) 224-3581